DANIEL
MAN OF GOD

Register This New Book

Benefits of Registering*

- ✓ FREE **replacements** of lost or damaged books

- ✓ FREE **audiobook** – *Pilgrim's Progress,*
  audiobook edition

- ✓ FREE information about new titles
  and other **freebies**

DANIEL
MAN OF GOD

Being a Man of Character
in a Babylon World

ORIGINAL TITLE: DANIEL THE PROPHET.
NEW, UPDATED EDITION.

D. L. Moody.

We love hearing from our readers. Please contact us at www.anekopress.com/questions-comments with any questions, comments, or suggestions.

Daniel Man of God – Dwight L. Moody

Revised Edition Copyright © 2018

First edition published 1884

Originally published by F. H. Revell,
148 & 150 Madison Street, Chicago

Cover Design: J. Martin

Cover Photography: Eric Isselee/Shutterstock

Editors: Sheila Wilkinson and Ruth Clark

Printed in China

Aneko Press

www.anekopress.com

Aneko Press, Life Sentence Publishing, and our logos are trademarks of

Life Sentence Publishing, Inc.
203 E. Birch Street
P.O. Box 652
Abbotsford, WI 54405

RELIGION / Christian Life / Spiritual Growth

Paperback ISBN: 978-1-62245-584-3

eBook ISBN: 978-1-62245-585-0

10   9   8   7   6   5   4   3

Available where books are sold

Contents

Daniel's Band

Standing by a purpose true,
   Heeding God's command,
Honor them, the faithful few,
   All hail to Daniel's Band!

     Dare to be a Daniel,
       Dare to stand alone,
       Dare to have a purpose firm,
       Dare to make it known.

Many mighty men are lost,
   Daring not to stand,
Who for God had been a host,
   By joining Daniel's Band.

Many giants, great and tall,
   Stalking through the land,
Headlong to the earth would fall,
   If met by Daniel's Band.

Hold the gospel banner high,
   On to vict'ry grand!
Satan and his host defy,
   And shout for Daniel's Band!

– Philip. P. Bliss (1873)

Chapter 1

Captives in Babylon

But Daniel made up his mind that he would
not defile himself with the king's choice
food or with the wine which he drank; so he
sought permission from the commander of
the officials that he might not defile himself.
– Daniel 1:8

I always delight to study the life of Daniel the prophet. The name *Daniel* means "God is my judge." God is my judge; the public is not my judge nor my fellow men, but God. So Daniel held himself responsible to God. Some may ask who Daniel was. About six hundred years before the time of Christ, the sins of the kings of Judah had brought the judgments of God upon them and upon the people. Jehoiakim had succeeded Jehoahaz, and Jehoiachin had succeeded Jehoiakim, and he was succeeded by Zedekiah. The record of each of these kings runs the same: *He did evil in the sight of the LORD* (1 Kings 15:26).

It is no wonder that in the days of Jehoiakim, about six hundred years before the time of Christ, Nebuchadnezzar, king of Babylon, was permitted by God to come up against Jerusalem and to lay siege against it and overcome it. It was probably at this time that Daniel, with some of the young princes, was carried away as a captive. A few years later, when Jehoiachin was king, Nebuchadnezzar came up against Jerusalem again and carried away many of the temple vessels and took several thousand captives.

And even later, when Zedekiah was king, Nebuchadnezzar came a third time against Jerusalem to besiege it. This time he burned the city with fire, broke down its walls, slaughtered many of the people, and probably carried away another batch of captives to the banks of the Euphrates (2 Kings 25:1-11).

Among the earlier captives taken by the king of Babylon in the days of Jehoiakim were four young men. Like Timothy in later times, they may have had godly mothers who taught them the law of the Lord. Or they may perhaps have been touched by the words of Jeremiah, the Weeping Prophet, whom God had sent to the people of Judah. So, even though the nation rejected the God of Israel, the God of Abraham, of Isaac, and of Moses, these young men took Him as their God; they received Him into their hearts.

Many may have mocked Jeremiah when he warned them and lifted up his voice against the sins of the people. They may have laughed at his tears and told him to his face that he was causing undue excitement, just as people say of earnest preachers today. But these four young men seemed to have listened to the prophet's voice, and they had the strength to stand for God.

In spite of their faithfulness, they were captives in Babylon. Nebuchadnezzar the king commanded that a certain number of the most promising of the young Jewish captives be chosen to be taught the Chaldean tongue and instructed in the learning of Babylon. The king further ordered that there should be portions of meat from his table set before them daily with a supply of the same wine as he himself drank; this was to continue for three years (Daniel 1:5).

At the end of three years these young men were to stand before the great monarch, the ruler over the whole world at that time. Daniel and his three young friends were among those thus selected. *But Daniel made up his mind that he would not defile himself with the king's choice food or with the wine which he drank; so he sought permission from the commander of the officials that he might not defile himself* (Daniel 1:8).

No young man ever goes from a country home to a large city or a great metropolis without serious temptations crossing his path on his entrance. And just at this turning point in a young man's life, as in Daniel's, must lie the secret of his success or his failure. The cause of many of the failures that we see in life is that men do not start right. Daniel, however, started right. He took his character with him to Babylon and was not ashamed of the religion of his father and his mother. He was not ashamed of the God of the Bible.

Among those heathen idolaters in Babylon, he was not ashamed to let his light shine. The young Hebrew captive took his stand for God as he entered the gate of Babylon, and doubtless he cried to God to keep him steadfast. And he needed to cry hard, for he had to face great difficulties, as we shall see.

Soon came a testing time. The king's edict went forth that these young men should eat the meat from the king's table. In all probability some of that food would consist of meats prohibited by the Levitical law – the flesh of animals, of birds, and of fish, which had been pronounced unclean and were consequently forbidden. Or, in the preparation, some portion might not have been thoroughly drained of the blood, concerning which it had been declared, *You are not to eat the blood of any flesh* (Leviticus 17:14). Some part of the food may have been presented as an offering to Bel or some other Babylonian god. Any one of these circumstances, or possibly all of them together, may have determined Daniel's course of action. I do not think it took young Daniel long to make up his mind. He *purposed in his heart* – in his heart, mark that! – *that he would not defile himself with the portion of the king's food.*

If some modern Christians could have advised Daniel, they might have said, "Don't act like that; don't set aside the king's meat; that is an act of Pharisaism. The moment you take your stand and say you will not eat it, you say in effect that you are better than other people." Oh yes, that is the kind of talk that is too often heard now. Men say, "When you are in Rome, you must do as the Roman does." Such people would

4

have pressed upon the poor young captive that he could not possibly stand for God in Babylon even though he might obey God's commandments while at home. He could not expect to carry his religion with him into the land of his captivity.

I can imagine men saying to Daniel, "Look here, young man, you are too puritanical. Don't be too particular; don't have too many religious scruples. Bear in mind you are not in Jerusalem now. You will have to get over these notions now that you are here in Babylon. You are not surrounded by friends and relatives. You are not a Jerusalem prince now. You are not surrounded by the royal family of Judah. You have been brought down from your high position. You are now a captive. And if the monarch hears about you refusing to eat the same meat that he eats or drink the same wine that he drinks, your head will soon roll off your shoulders. You had better be a little more politically correct."

> This young man had devotion and religion deep down in his heart, and that is the right place for it.

But this young man had devotion and religion deep down in his heart, and that is the right place for it. That is where it will grow, have power, and regulate life. Daniel had not joined the company of the "church," the faithful few in Jerusalem, to attain a position in society; that was not the reason. It was because of the love he had for the Lord God of Israel.

I can imagine the astonishment of that officer, Melzar, when Daniel told him he could not eat the king's meat or drink his wine. "Why, what do you mean? Is there anything wrong with it? Why, it is the best the land can produce!"

"No," said Daniel, "there is nothing wrong with it in that way, but take it away; I cannot eat it." Then Melzar tried to reason Daniel out of his scruples; but no, there stood the prophet, young though he was at that time, firm as a rock.

So, thank God, this young Hebrew and his three friends said they would not eat the meat or drink the wine; they requested that the portions be taken away and they endeavored to persuade the overseer to bring them vegetables instead (Daniel 1:12-13).

"Take away this wine, and take away this meat. Give us vegetables and water." The prince of the eunuchs probably trembled for fear of the consequences. But, yielding to their appeal, he eventually consented to let them have vegetables and water for ten days. And lo, at the end of the ten days his fears were dispelled, for the faces of Daniel and his young friends *seemed better and they were fatter than all the youths who had been eating the king's choice food* (Daniel 1:15). The four young men did not have noses like those of many men in our streets, as red as if they were going to blossom. It is God's truth – and Daniel and his friends tested it – that cold water with a clear conscience is better than wine. They had a clear conscience, and the smile of God was upon them. The Lord had blessed their obedience, and the four Hebrew youths were allowed to have their own way. In God's time they were brought into favor, not only with the officer over them but also with the court and the king.

Daniel thought more of his principles than he did of earthly honor or the esteem of men. Right was right with him. He was going to do right that day and let the tomorrows take care of themselves. That firmness of purpose in the strength of God was the secret of his success. Right there, that very moment, he overcame. And from that hour, from that moment, he could go on conquering and to conquer, because he had started right.

A man is often lost because he does not start right. He makes a bad start. A young man comes from his country home and enters upon city life; temptation arises, and he becomes unfaithful to his principles. He meets with some scoffing, sneering man who jeers at him because he goes to a church service, reads his Bible, or prays to God – the same God to whom Daniel prayed in Babylon. And the young man might prove to be weak-kneed and cannot stand the scoffs, the sneers, and the jeers of his companions. So he becomes untrue to his principles and gives them up. *Do not be deceived: Bad company corrupts good morals* (1 Corinthians 15:33).

A man is often lost because he does not start right.

I want to say that when a young man makes a wrong start, in ninety-nine cases out of a hundred, it is ruin to him. The first game of chance, the first betting transaction, the first false entry in the books, the first quarter-dollar taken from the cash box or the till, or the first night spent in evil company – any of these may prove the turning point; any of these may represent a wrong start.

If any persons could have claimed a good excuse for

being unfaithful to their principles, these four young men might have. They had been torn away from the associations of their childhood and their youth; they had been taken away from the religious influences that centered in Jerusalem, away from the temple services and sacrifices, and they had been taken to Babylon to associate with the idols and idolaters, the wise men and soothsayers. The whole nation was against them, but they stood against the current of the whole world.

God Was with Them

And when a man, for the sake of principle and conscience, goes against the current of the whole world, God is with him, and he need not stop to consider what the consequences will be. God has said, *Have I not commanded you? Be strong and courageous! Do not tremble or be dismayed, for the LORD your God is with you wherever you go* (Joshua 1:9). Right is right.

But our testimony for God is not limited to a single act; it has to last all through our lives. So we must not imagine for a moment that Daniel had only one trial to undergo. The word to the Lord's servants is the same in all ages: *Be faithful until death* (Revelation 2:10).

This city of Babylon was a vast place. It might have been the largest city the world has ever seen. It is said to have been sixty miles around and is understood to have consisted of an area of two hundred square miles.[1]

---

1   "Herodotus gives the circumference of Babylon as sixty miles, the whole forming a quadrangle, of which each side was fifteen miles. M. Oppert confirms this by examinations on the spot, which show an area within the wall of two hundred square miles" *(Fausset's Bible Cyclopedia*, p. 67). A clearer idea of the enormous extent of Babylon will be formed if we understand that it probably occupied an area

A line drawn through the city in either direction would measure fifteen miles. The walls had an elevation of three hundred and fifty feet; they would therefore be nearly on a level with the dome of St. Paul's Cathedral in London. The breadth of the walls was over eighty feet, and eight chariots could run abreast on the top. Babylon was like Chicago – so flat that for ornamentation men had to construct artificial mounds. Like Chicago in another way, the products of vast regions flowed right into and through it.

---

nearly *double* the size of modern London. It must not, however, be supposed that Babylon contained a population comparable with that of London. The inhabitants of the former city probably numbered 1.2 million.

Chapter 2

Hearing from God

Nebuchadnezzar had dreams; and his
spirit was troubled and his sleep left him.
– Daniel 2:1

A few years later we hear of Daniel again, but under new conditions. The king of Babylon had a dream, and his dream greatly disturbed him. He musters before him the magicians, the astrologers, the soothsayers, and the Chaldeans (or learned men), and requests the interpretation of this night vision from them. He either cannot or will not narrate to them the incidents of the vision, but he demands an explanation without detailing what he has seen in his dream. *The command from me is firm: if you do not make known to me the dream and its interpretation, you will be torn limb from limb and your houses will be made a rubbish heap* (Daniel 2:5).

That was a pretty unreasonable demand. It is true that he offered them rewards and honors if they succeeded, but of course they failed. And they admitted their failure. *The Chaldeans answered the king and said, "There is not a man on earth who could declare the matter for the king, inasmuch as no great king or ruler has ever asked anything like this of any magician, conjurer or Chaldean. Moreover, the thing which the king demands is difficult, and there is no one else who could declare it to the king except gods, whose dwelling place is not with mortal flesh"* (Daniel 2:10-11).

Except the angels of God. The king's men knew that men themselves didn't have the understanding or discernment needed to tell the king what his dream had been – they knew that only God had that power, and rightly told the king so.

There is not a man on earth who could declare the matter for the king. But they didn't think of Daniel, who know God and therefore could depend on God to do far and above what natural man could. *Because of this the king became indignant and very furious and gave orders to destroy all the wise men of Babylon. So the decree went forth that the wise men should be slain; and they looked for Daniel and his friends to kill them* (Daniel 2:12-13).

The king's officer came to Daniel, but Daniel was not afraid. The officer said to him, "You are classed among the wise men, and our orders are to take you out and execute you."

The young Hebrew captive responded, *"For what reason is the decree from the king so urgent?"* . . . *So Daniel went in and requested of the king that he would give him time, in order that he might declare the interpretation to the king* (Daniel 2:15-16).

He had read the law of Moses, and he was one of those who believed that what Moses had written concerning secret things was true: *The secret things belong to the LORD our God, but the things revealed belong to us and to our sons forever* (Deuteronomy 29:29). He probably said to himself, "My God knows that secret, and I will trust Him to reveal it to me." And he may have called his three friends together and held a prayer meeting – perhaps the first prayer meeting ever held in Babylon. They dealt with the threatening message of the king of Babylon just as Hezekiah had

> Daniel's faith was strong, so he could sleep calmly in the prospect of death.

dealt with the threatening letter of the king of Assyria a hundred years before. They *spread it out before the LORD* (2 Kings 19:14). They prayed that this secret might be revealed to them. After they had prayed and made their request to God, the answer did not come immediately, so they went to bed and fell asleep.

I do not think that you or I would have slept much, if we thought that our heads were in danger of coming off in the morning. Daniel slept, for we are told the matter was revealed to him in a dream or night vision. Daniel's faith was strong, so he could sleep calmly in the prospect of death. If his friends did not sleep through the night, they were probably praying.

Daniel Stands before the King

In the morning, Daniel poured out his heart in thanksgiving. He *blessed the God of heaven* (Daniel 2:19). He had got into the spirit of Psalm 103: *Bless the LORD, O my soul, and all that is within me, bless His holy name* (Psalm 103:1). Paul and Silas had the same spirit of thanksgiving when they were in the prison at Philippi, for *Paul and Silas were praying and singing hymns of praise to God, and the prisoners were listening to them* (Acts 16:25).

Daniel made his way to the palace, went to the guard room, and said to the officer, *"Take me into the king's presence, and I will declare the interpretation to the king"* (Daniel 2:24). He stood in the presence of Nebuchadnezzar, and like Joseph before Pharaoh (Genesis 41:16), before proceeding to unfold the dream, he gave glory to God: *There is a God in heaven who reveals mysteries* (Daniel 2:28). Daniel took his place as a nobody; he himself was nothing. He did not wish the king to think highly of him. That is the very highest type of devotion – when a man hides himself out of the way and seeks to exalt his God and lift up his Redeemer, not himself. Then Daniel proceeded to describe the dream: *You, O king, were looking and behold, there was a single great statue; that statue, which was large and of extraordinary splendor, was standing in front of you, and its appearance was awesome* (Daniel 2:31).

I can imagine how the king's eyes flashed out at those opening words, and I can fancy him crying out, "Yes, that is it! The whole thing comes back to me now!"

> *The head of that statue was made of fine gold, its breast and its arms of silver, its belly and its thighs of bronze, its legs of iron, its feet partly of iron and partly of clay* (Daniel 2:32-33).

"Yes, that is it exactly," the king might have responded. "I recollect all that now. But surely there was something more."

> So Daniel went on: *You continued looking until a stone was cut out without hands, and it struck the statue on its feet of iron and clay and crushed them. This was the dream; now we will tell its interpretation before the king* (Daniel 2:34, 36).

And then, amidst deathlike stillness, Daniel went on to unfold the interpretation, and he told the king that the golden head of the great image was none other than himself. *You are the head of gold* (Daniel 2:38). He went on to tell of another kingdom that would arise – not so beautiful, but stronger, as silver is stronger but less pure than gold, that described the Medo-Persian empire (silver tarnishes, while gold does not). But the arms of silver were to overthrow the head of gold.

Daniel himself lived to see the day when that part of the prophetic dream came to pass. He lived to see Cyrus overthrow the Chaldean power. He lived to see the scepter of the empire pass into the hands of the Medes and Persians. And after them came a mighty Grecian conqueror, Alexander the Great, who overthrew the Persian dynasty, and for a while Greece ruled the world. Then came the Caesars who founded the empire of Rome, which was symbolized by the legs of iron, the mightiest power the world had ever known, but containing many impurities (iron rusts very easily). For centuries Rome sat on those seven hills and ruled over the nations of the earth. And then, in its turn, the

Roman power was broken, and the mighty empire split up into ten kingdoms corresponding to the ten toes of the prophetic figure.

I believe in the literal fulfillment of Daniel's God-given words and in the sure fulfillment of the final prophecy of the stone *cut out, not with hands*, that by and by will grind the kingdoms of this world into dust and bring in the kingdom of peace.

Even though the feet were of clay, there was some of the strength of the iron remaining in them. At the present day, we are down to the toes – and even to the very tips of these. Soon, very soon, the collision may occur and then will come the end. The "stone cut out without hands" is surely coming – and it may be very soon.

What did Ezekiel say when he prophesied within a few years of the time of this very vision? *Remove the turban and take off the crown; . . . A ruin, a ruin, a ruin, I will make it. This also will be no more until He comes whose right it is, and I will give it to Him* (Ezekiel 21:26-27).

What did the apostle Paul say? *The appearing of our Lord Jesus Christ, which He will bring about at the proper time -He who is the blessed and only Sovereign, the King of kings and Lord of lords; . . . To Him be honor and eternal dominion* (1 Timothy 6:14-16).

Yes, the fifth monarchy is coming, and it may be very soon. Hail to the fifth monarch, who will rule the world in righteousness and reign *from the River to the ends of the earth* (Psalm 72:8). Shortly the cry, "Christ is come!" will be ringing throughout the earth. It is only a little while. Cheer up, ye children of God; our King will be back by and by! And to those who have not yet given their hearts to Christ, I would say, Lose no time! If you want to have a part in that coming kingdom of the Lord, you had better press into it now while the door is open. Soon, "Too late! too late!" will be the cry.

When King Nebuchadnezzar heard the full description of his dream and listened to its interpretation, he was satisfied that at last he had found a really wise man. He gave Daniel many great gifts and raised him to a position near the throne, just as Pharaoh had raised Joseph ages before. And when Daniel was raised to position and power, he did not forget his friends; he requested of the king that they be promoted, so they also were put in positions of honor and trust. God blessed them specifically, and He kept them true to Him in their prosperity, as they had been in their adversity.

> It is better for a man to be right with God, even if he holds no position down here.

From that moment Daniel became a great man. He was set over the province of Babylon. He was lifted right out of bondage – right out of servitude. He was a young man, probably not more than twenty-two years old, and there he was over a mighty empire. He was practically made ruler over the whole of the then-known world.

And God will exalt us also when the right time comes. We don't need to try to promote ourselves; we don't need to struggle for position. Let God put us in our true places. It is better for a man to be right with God, even if he holds no position down here. Then he can look up and know that God is pleased with him. That is enough.

Fight the Good Fight

How goes the fight with thee?
  The life-long battle with all evil things?
Thine no low strife, and thine no selfish aim;
  It is the war of giants and of kings.

Goes the fight well with thee?
  This living fight with death and death's dark power?
Is not the stronger than the strong one near;
  With thee and *for* thee in the fiercest hour?

Dread not the din and smoke,
  The stifling poison of the fiery air;
Courage! It is the battle of thy God;
  Go, and for Him learn how to do and dare!

What though ten thousand fall!
  And the red field with the dear dead be strewn;
Grasp but more bravely thy bright shield and sword;
  Fight to the last, although thou fight'st alone.

What though ten thousand faint,
  Desert, or yield, or in weak terror flee!
Heed not the panic of the multitude;
  Thine be the Captain's watchword – Victory!
    – Dr. H. Bonar (1868)

Chapter 3

Abstaining from Idol Worship

*Nebuchadnezzar the king made an image
of gold, the height of which was sixty cubits
and its width six cubits; he set it up on the
plain of Dura in the province of Babylon.*
– Daniel 3:1

Time went on, possibly several years, and a crisis
occurred. Whether or not that dream of a gigantic human figure continued to haunt Nebuchadnezzar,
we do not know, but it is quite possible that the dream
may have suggested Nebuchadnezzar's next action. He
ordered the construction of an immense image. It was to
be of gold – not simply gilded, but actually of pure gold.

Gold is a symbol of prosperity, and at this time
Babylon was prosperous. Likewise, in the prosperous
days of Jerusalem, gold was abundant, and some of the
precious metal that was carried away as the spoils of
war from the Jewish capital may have been used in the

construction of this statue of gold. It was of colossal size – over ninety feet high and between nine and ten feet wide. This gigantic image was set up in the plain of Dura near to the city. Nebuchadnezzar probably wanted to gratify his imperial vanity by inaugurating a universal religion.

When the time came for the dedication, however, Daniel was not there. He may have been away in Egypt or in one of the many provinces attending to the affairs of the empire. If he had been in Babylon, we would surely have heard of him. Representatives, princes, governors, counselors, high secretaries, and judges were ordered to be present at the dedication of the statue. What a gathering that morning! It was fashionable to be seen that morning, driving to the plain of Dura. All the great people and all the rich people were to be there.

Hark! The trumpet sounded; the royal messenger shouted, *"To you the command is given, O peoples, nations and men of every language, that at the moment you hear the sound of the horn, flute, lyre, trigon, psaltery, bagpipe and all kinds of music, you are to fall down and worship the golden image that Nebuchadnezzar the king has set up. But whoever does not fall down and worship shall immediately be cast into the midst of a furnace of blazing fire"* (Daniel 3:4-6).

Perhaps a part of the ceremony consisted in the unveiling of the statue. One thing is certain: at the given signal all the people were required to fall to the earth and worship.

But in the law of God there was something against that. God's voice had spoken at Sinai, and God's finger had written on the table of stone – *You shall have no other gods before Me* (Exodus 20:3). God's law went directly against the king's decree. Though Daniel was not on the plain of Dura, his influence was there. He had influenced his three friends – Shadrach, Meshach, and Abednego. They were there, and they were inspired by the same spirit as Daniel. Their position brought them to this place at the hour of the dedication.

Remember, no man can be true to God and live for Him without at some time or other being unpopular in this world. Those men who try to live for both worlds fail miserably, for at some time or other the collision is sure to come. Would all of us have advised Daniel's three friends to do the right thing at any cost? Aren't there some of us who have so little backbone that we would have counseled these three to just bow down a little, so that no one would notice – to merely bow down, but not to worship?

> No man can be true to God and live for Him without at some time or other being unpopular in this world.

When Daniel and his friends first came to Babylon, they perceived that the two worlds – the present world and the world to come – would collide, and they chose the world to come; they chose things unseen. They did not determine for the present time only, but they took their stand immediately. Even if it cost them their lives, what did that matter? It would only hasten them to their glory, and they would receive the greater reward. They took their stand for God and for the unseen world.

The faithful three utterly refused to bend the knee to a god of gold.

A terrible penalty was associated with disobedience to the king's command: *whoever does not fall down and worship shall immediately be cast into the midst of a furnace of blazing fire* (Daniel 3:6). This was not a mere empty threat. It was a sentence in harmony with the character and practice of the ferocious and cruel king as the prophet Jeremiah recorded: *May the LORD make you like Zedekiah and like Ahab, whom the king of Babylon roasted in the fire* (Jeremiah 29:22).[2]

How many would cry out in this city – in every city – "Give me gold, give me money, and I will do anything!" Some people may say that the men of Nebuchadnezzar's day shouldn't have bowed to a golden idol, but they themselves are doing that very thing every day. Money is their god; social position is their golden image. Plenty of men today bow to the golden image that the world has set up. "Give me gold! Give me gold, and you may have heaven. Give me position, and you may have the world to come. Give me worldly honor, and I will sell out my hopes of heaven. Give me the thirty pieces of silver, and I will give you Christ." That is the cry of the world today.

And now the order is given – very probably by the king himself – that the bands should strike up just like bands of music play on special occasions today. The

---

2   It is well for us to remember that the burning of living beings has not been confined to a distant country and a barbarous age. Three hundred years ago, an English queen, whose name has become a proverb, during her short reign of five years and five months, caused no fewer than 277 persons to be roasted alive in England – *of whom fifty-five were women and four were children.*

music could be heard from far away, and when the first notes burst forth, all were to bow to the golden statue. Earth's great ones and mighty ones bowed at the king's command. But there were three with stiff knees that did not bend. Those were Daniel's three friends, who knew that to do the king's bidding would be to break the law of their God. They chose to not fall down and worship. At the king's command, they had come to the dedication;

These are the kind of servants God wants – men who will stand up bravely and fearlessly for Him.

there might be nothing wrong in that, but they would not bow down. They were too strong in the backbone for that. They remembered the command, *You shall have no other gods before Me.* These are the kind of servants God wants – men who will stand up bravely and fearlessly for Him.

Like all the servants of the Lord and all who walk in the atmosphere of heaven, these three Hebrews had enemies who bore them a bitter grudge. Very possibly they thought these three had undue preference in being promoted to office. So there were some others, besides the three young Hebrews, who did not worship as commanded. Do you know what they did? They watched Shadrach, Meshach, and Abednego. If they themselves had bowed their faces to the ground according to Nebuchadnezzar's command, they would not have seen that Daniel's three friends refused to bow. They would not have seen the three young Hebrews standing up, erect and straight. Those Chaldeans looked out of the corners of their eyes and watched the three young men.

These young Jews had carried themselves and had lived in Babylon in such a way that their watchers felt sure they would not bow to the statue. They knew that the three would not sacrifice their principles. They would go as far as it was lawful in obeying the king's commands, but a time would come when they would draw the line. When the commands of the earthly sovereign came in conflict with the commands of the God of heaven, they would not yield. The watchers watched, but the young men did not bow.

Thank God, they had backbone, if you will allow me that expression. Something held their knees firm; they would not give in; there they stood as firm as rock. They stood *strong in the Lord and in the strength of His might* (Ephesians 6:10). They did not get halfway down to make believe that they were going to worship the image. There was nothing of that kind; they stood up erect and firm.

Some of those Chaldeans wished to get rid of these young Hebrews. Perhaps they wanted their places, or they were after their offices. Men have been the same in all ages. No doubt, there were a good many men in Babylon who wanted their posts. These three men had high positions; there was much honor attached to their offices, so their enemies wanted to oust them and succeed to their offices. It is a very bad state of things when men try to pull others down in order to obtain their places, but there is a good deal of that in this world. Many a man has had his character blasted and ruined by some person who wanted to step into his place and position.

So away went those men to the king to disclose information. They duly rendered the salutation: *O king, live for ever.* Then they went on to tell him of those rebellious Hebrews who would not obey the king's order. *There are certain Jews . . . these men, O king, have disregarded you; they do not serve your gods or worship the golden image which you have set up* (Daniel 3:12).

"Three men in my kingdom who will not obey me!" Nebuchadnezzar might have roared. "No! Who are they? What are their names?"

"Why, those three Hebrew slaves whom you set over us – Shadrach, Meshach, and Abednego. When the music started, they did not bow; it was talked about all around; the people know it. If you allow them to go unpunished, it will not be long before your law will be perfectly worthless."

I can imagine the king was almost speechless with rage as he commanded that the men be brought before him.

> *Is it true, Shadrach, Meshach and Abednego, that you do not serve my gods or worship the golden image that I have set up?* (Daniel 3:14).

"It is true, quite true," perhaps Shadrach answered. "Quite true, O king."

One last chance Nebuchadnezzar resolved to give them. *Now if you are ready, at the moment you hear the sound of the horn, flute, lyre, trigon, psaltery and bagpipe and all kinds of music, to fall down and worship the image that I have made, very well. But if you do not worship, you will immediately be cast into the midst of a furnace of blazing fire; and what god is there who can deliver you out of my hands?* (Daniel 3:15).

That is pretty plain speaking, is it not? There is no mincing or smoothing over matters. Do this, and you live; don't do it, and you die. But the threat that the king made had little terror for them. They turned *and replied to the king, "O Nebuchadnezzar, we do not need to give you an answer concerning this matter. If it be so, our God whom we serve is able to deliver us from the furnace of blazing fire; and He will deliver us out of your hand, O king. But even if He does not, let it be known to you, O king, that we are not going to serve your gods or worship the golden image that you have set up"* (Daniel 3:16-18).

And that is plain speaking too. The king of Babylon had not been accustomed to someone talking to him like that. And he did not like it. We are told he was *full of fury.*

These Hebrew men spoke respectfully but firmly. And note, they did not absolutely say that God *would* deliver them from the burning fiery furnace, but they declared that He was *able* to deliver them. They had no doubt about His ability to do it. They believed that He would do it, but they did not hide from themselves the possibility of Nebuchadnezzar being allowed to carry out his threats.

Still, that did not greatly move them. *But if not* – if in His incomprehensible purposes, He allowed them to suffer, their resolve would be the same: *we are not going to serve your gods or worship the golden image that you have set up.* They were not afraid to pass from the presence of the king of Babylon into the presence of the King of Kings. Those men had courage. I wonder if three such brave men could be found in New York, or in Boston, or in Baltimore, or in Chicago today. How settled they were in their minds! Thank God for such courage! Thank God for such boldness! A few such men, brave and fearless for God, could soon turn the world upside down. Today they would be considered fanatics; they would be advised to bow outwardly but not "worship" the image. But even the suggestion of worshipping an image was too much for them; they were determined to avoid even the appearance of evil.

> A few men, brave and fearless for God, could soon turn the world upside down.

Look at the king's reaction. I can imagine him in his fury, trembling like an aspen leaf and turning pale as death with rage. *He answered by giving orders to heat the furnace seven times more than it was usually heated. He commanded certain valiant warriors who were in his army to tie up Shadrach, Meshach and Abed-nego in order to cast them into the furnace of blazing fire. Then these men were tied up in their trousers, their coats, their caps and their other clothes, and were cast into the midst of the furnace of blazing fire* (Daniel 3:19-21).

The command was instantly executed, and they were hurled into the terrible blaze. The fire was so furious that the flames consumed the officers who thrust them in.[3] The three young Hebrews *fell into the midst*

---

3   Those who have stood upon the "feed" platform of a great iron-smelting

of the furnace of blazing fire still tied up and it seemed as if they would not be saved (Daniel 3:23). From his royal seat, the king peered out and looked to see the rebels burnt to ashes.

But when Nebuchadnezzar gazed upon the furnace, expecting the gratification of his vengeance, to his great amazement, he saw the men walking about in the midst of the flames. They walked – they were not running – as if in the midst of green pastures or beside still waters. There was no difference in them except that their bonds were burnt off. Ah, it does my heart good to think that the worst the devil can do is to burn off the bonds of God's children. If Christ is with us, the direst afflictions can only loosen our earthly bonds and set us free to soar higher.

Nebuchadnezzar beheld strange things that day. Through the flames, he saw four men walking in the midst of the fire, although only three had been cast in. How was this? The Great Shepherd in yonder heaven saw that three of His lambs were in trouble, and He leaped down, right into the fiery furnace. And when Nebuchadnezzar looked in, he saw the form of a fourth man.

> *"Was it not three men we cast bound into*
> *the midst of the fire?" They replied to the*
> *king, "Certainly, O king." He said, "Look! I*

---

furnace and felt the enormous pressure of the atmosphere as it rushes forward to fill up the vacuum from the air of the furnace, and have experienced the *suck* or *draw* towards the edge of the platform that is felt when the furnace doors are thrown open, will easily understand how perilous a close approach to the mouth would be and how easily Nebuchadnezzar's *mighty men* would be drawn into the power of the flames if they ventured within the range of that furnace.

*see four men loosed and walking about in
the midst of the fire without harm, and the
appearance of the fourth is like a son of the
gods!"* (Daniel 3:24-25)

It was doubtless the Son of God.[4] That Great Shepherd
of the sheep saw that three of His true servants were
in peril, and He came from His Father's presence and
His Father's bosom to be with them. He had watched
that terrible scene of the attempt to burn the faithful
three, and His tender, pitying eye saw that men were
condemned to death because of their loyalty to Him.

With one great leap He sprang from the Father's
presence, from His palace in glory, right into the fiery
furnace, and was by their side
before the heat of the fire could
come near them. Jesus was with
His servants as the flames encir-
cled them, and not a hair of their
heads was singed. They were not scorched, and not even
the smell of fire clung to them. I can imagine them
chanting: *When you pass through the waters, I will be
with you; And through the rivers, they will not overflow
you. When you walk through the fire, you will not be
scorched, Nor will the flame burn you* (Isaiah 43:2).

**God can take care
of us when we pass
through the fires.**

God can take care of us when we pass through the
waters; God can take care of us when we pass through
the fires. God is *able* to take care of us, if only we will

---

4   That the fourth was the Lord Jesus Christ, He who appeared to
     Abraham and wrestled with Jacob, has been an accepted truth with
     almost everyone who ministers the Word. It is only fair to say that
     in the original text, the definite article is absent, and the sentence
     reads, "like a son of gods."

stand up for Him. God *will* take care of us, if only we will stand up for Him. Young man, honor God, and God will honor you. What you have to do is take your stand upon God's side. If you have to go against the whole world, take that stand. Dare to do right; dare to be true; dare to be honest. Let the consequences be what they may.

You may have to forfeit your situation because you cannot, and will not, do something that your employer requires you to do, but that your conscience tells you is wrong. Give up your situation then, rather than give up your principles. If your employer requires you to sell goods by means of misrepresentation, fraud, or falsehood, give up your situation and say, "I would rather die a pauper; I would rather die in a poorhouse than be unfaithful to my principles." That is the kind of stuff those men were made of. These glorious heroes braved even death because God was with them. Oh friends, we want to be Christians with the same backbone – men and women who are prepared to stand up for the right and heed not what the world may say or what the world may think.

Then Nebuchadnezzar came near to the door of the furnace of blazing fire; he responded and said, "Shadrach, Meshach and Abed-nego, come out, you servants of the Most High God, and come here!" (Daniel 3:26). And they walked out, untouched by the fire. They came out like giants in their conscious strength. Imagine how the princes, the governors, the counselors, and the great men crowded around them to see such an unheard-of sight. Their garments showed no trace of fire; their hair was not even singed. It was as if God was teaching them that He guards *even the very hairs of your head* (Luke 12:7).

Nebuchadnezzar had defied God and had been conquered. God had proved Himself able to deliver His servants out of the king's hand. Nebuchadnezzar accepted his defeat and made this decree: *That any people, nation or tongue that speaks anything offensive against the God of Shadrach, Meshach and Abed-nego shall be torn limb from limb and their houses reduced to a rubbish heap, inasmuch as there is no other god who is able to deliver in this way* (Daniel 3:29).

Then Nebuchadnezzar promoted these three witnesses to a higher place and position and put greater honor upon them. God stood by them because they had stood by Him. God desires us to do something just because it is right and not because it is popular. The outcome may seem to lead to death, but do the right thing, and if we stand firm, God will work everything for the best.

That is the last we hear of these three men. God sent them to Babylon to shine, and they did shine.

Living! Working! Waiting!

Who would not *live* for Jesus,
    Rejoicing, glad and free?
The music of a ransomed life
    Is all He asks from thee.

Who would not *work* for Jesus,
    When service is but song?
The rippling of a stream of love
    That bears thy soul along.

Who would not *die* for Jesus,
    When death is victory?
The grand, o'ershadowing portal-gate
    Guarding eternity.

Who would not *wait* for Jesus?
    And waiting, sweetly sing,
Hushing their heart with promises
    While tarrying for their King.
        – Eva Travers Poole

Chapter 4

Pride Goes Before Destruction

I, Nebuchadnezzar, was at ease in my house and flourishing in my palace. I saw a dream and it made me fearful; and these fantasies as I lay on my bed and the visions in my mind kept alarming me. – Daniel 4:4-5

After a time, Nebuchadnezzar had another dream. Surely, one would think this man would see God's hand at last. How many signs and wonders had he seen that worked to convince him of God's mighty power? This time Nebuchadnezzar remembered the particulars of the dream; they stood out vivid and clear in his mind.

Again he called in the four classes of men that he counted on to make dark things light and hidden things plain. He recounted to them the incidents of this dream, but the magicians, the astrologers, the Chaldeans, and the soothsayers all failed to tell him the interpretation. When they had been called upon to interpret his former dream, they had all stood silent. And they stood silent again as Nebuchadnezzar revealed the second dream to them. There was something in these dreams of the king that stopped their mouths that were usually so ready with some plausible interpretation. But with these royal dreams, it was no use; they were beaten.

It would appear that Nebuchadnezzar had almost forgotten the man who had recounted to him his former dream and given its interpretation. He said, *But finally Daniel came in before me.* And he proceeded to address Daniel by his Chaldean name of Belteshazzar:

> *O Belteshazzar, chief of the magicians, since I know that a spirit of the holy gods is in you and no mystery baffles you, tell me the visions of my dream which I have seen, along with its interpretation. Now these were the visions in my mind as I lay on my bed: I was looking, and behold, there was a tree in the midst of the earth and its height was great. The tree grew large and became strong and its height reached to the sky, and it was visible to the end of the whole earth. Its foliage was beautiful and its fruit abundant, and in it was food for all. The beasts of the field found shade under it, and the birds of the sky dwelt in its branches, and all living creatures fed themselves from it.*
>
> *I was looking in the visions in my mind as I lay*

on my bed, and behold, an angelic watcher, a holy one, descended from heaven. He shouted out and spoke as follows: "Chop down the tree and cut off its branches, Strip off its foliage and scatter its fruit; Let the beasts flee from under it and the birds from its branches. Yet leave the stump with its roots in the ground, but with a band of iron and bronze around it in the new grass of the field; And let him be drenched with the dew of heaven, and let him share with the beasts in the grass of the earth. Let his mind be changed from that of a man and let a beast's mind be given to him, and let seven periods of time pass over him."

This sentence is by the decree of the angelic watchers and the decision is a command of the holy ones, in order that the living may know that the Most High is ruler over the realm of mankind, and bestows it on whom He wishes and sets over it the lowliest of men. This is the dream which I, King Nebuchadnezzar, have seen. Now you, Belteshazzar, tell me its inter-pretation, inasmuch as none of the wise men of my kingdom is able to make known to me the interpretation; but you are able, for a spirit of the holy gods is in you. (Daniel 4:9-18)

As soon as the prophet appeared on the scene the king felt sure that he would get the meaning of the dream. For a time, Daniel stood still and motionless. Did his heart fail him? The record simply says he *was appalled for a while as his thoughts alarmed him* (Daniel 4:19). He saw what was meant by the royal dream – that the king was to have a terrible fall and that the kingdom was to be taken from this proud monarch for a season. The immediate words rushed to his lips, but he hated to let them out. He did not want to tell Nebuchadnezzar that his kingdom and his mind were both about to depart from him, and that he was to wander about and eat grass like a beast.

The king also hesitated; a dark foreboding got the better of his curiosity for a time. But he braced himself to hear the worst, and in kind words asked Daniel to proceed and tell all he knew. So Daniel broke the silence. He did not smooth over the matter but spoke plainly. There and then he preached righteousness to the king. A very good sermon it was too that he preached. If we had more of the same sort now, it would be better for us. He entreated the king: *May my advice be pleasing to you: break away now from your sins by doing righteousness and from your iniquities by showing mercy to the poor, in case there may be a prolonging of your prosperity* (Daniel 4:27).

Perhaps for encouragement he told him how the king of Nineveh had repented at the preaching of Jonah more than two centuries earlier. Then Daniel unfolded the full meaning of the dream. He told the king that the great and strong tree symbolized Nebuchadnezzar himself, and that just as the tree was hewn down and destroyed, so would he be stripped of power and robbed of strength. Daniel told him that he would be driven from among men and would have to live and eat with the beasts of the field. But the kingdom would revert to him in the end, just as the great watchman had spared the stump of the tree.

Repentance might have deferred, or even averted, the threatened calamity. But at that time Nebuchadnezzar repented not. And twelve months afterwards, the king, heedless of the prophetic warning and puffed up with pride, walked upon the corridors of his great palace and looked out at the city's vast extent; he gazed at those hanging gardens, which became one of the wonders of the world, and said, *Is this not Babylon the great, which I myself have built as a royal residence by the might of my power and for the glory of my majesty?* (Daniel 4:30).

> It would not take fifteen minutes today to prove that the world has gone clean mad – and the mass of professing Christians too.

A voice from heaven instantly spoke: *Sovereignty has been removed from you* (Daniel 4:31). And then and there God touched his reason; it reeled and tottered on its throne and fled. He was driven from among men; he dwelt with animals; his body was wet with the dew of heaven. This greatest of princes had gone clean mad.

It would not take fifteen minutes today to prove that the world has gone clean mad – and the mass of professing Christians too. Don't men think and talk as if everything were done by their own power? Isn't God completely forgotten? Don't men neglect every warning that in mercy He sends? Yes, men are mad, and nothing short of it.

Nebuchadnezzar's Repentance

But Nebuchadnezzar's kingdom had not passed away from him permanently; according to the prophet's word, at the close of the *seven times,* his understanding returned to him, and he resumed his throne and his authority. His counselors and officers gathered around him again. He regained his power, and he was a very different man. Truly, the king's reason had returned to him, and he was possessed with a very different spirit. He sent forth a new proclamation that gave honor to the Most High and exalted the God of heaven. The closing words of Daniel 4 show Nebuchadnezzar's repentance and tend to prove that Daniel had brought this mighty king to God.

It is interesting to consider the different proclamations of Nebuchadnezzar and note the change that takes place in them. He sent out one proclamation that instructed what other people ought to do and how they should serve the God of these Hebrews. But he did not truly understand the truth until this point. Here is his closing proclamation:

> *At the end of that period, I, Nebuchadnezzar, raised my eyes toward heaven and my reason returned to me, and I blessed the Most High and praised and honored Him who lives forever; For His dominion is an everlasting dominion, and His kingdom endures from generation to generation: At that time my reason returned to me. And my majesty and splendor were restored to me for the*

> *glory of my kingdom, and my counselors and my nobles began seeking me out; so I was reestablished in my sovereignty, and surpassing greatness was added to me. Now I, Nebuchadnezzar, praise, exalt and honor the King of heaven, for all His works are true and His ways just, and He is able to humble those who walk in pride.* (Daniel 4:34, 36-37)

When you see a man praising God, it is a good sign. The earlier edict said much about other people's duty towards the God of the Hebrews, but nothing about what the king himself should do. Oh, let us secure personal love and personal praise. That is needed in the church in the present day.

Nebuchadnezzar passed from the stage; this is the last record we have of him. But we may surely hope that, like that of the Corinthians, his was a *repentance to salvation not to be repented of* (2 Corinthians 7:10 KJV). And if this is so, we may well believe that today Nebuchadnezzar the king and Daniel the captive will be walking the crystal pavement of heaven arm in arm together and may be talking about the old times in Babylon.

When you see a man praising God, it is a good sign.

Now, if the young prophet had been of a vacillating character, if he had been of a willowy growth, easily shaken by every wind, and if he had not stood there in that city like a great oak, do you think he would have won this mighty monarch to his religion and his God? As a result of that young man going to that heathen city and standing firm for his God, the God of the Bible, the Lord honored him and gave him that mighty monarch as a star in his crown. We may fairly say that King Nebuchadnezzar was led to the God of the Hebrews through the faith of this Hebrew's love – just because he had a purpose firm and dared to make it known.

The Master's Service

Service of Jesus! Oh, service of sweetness!
    There are no bonds in that service for me;
Full of delight and most perfect completeness,
    Evermore His, yet so joyously free!

Service of Jesus! Oh, service of power!
    Sharing His glory, while sharing His shame;
All the best blessings the Master can shower
    Rest on the servant exalting His name.

Service of Jesus! Oh, service joy-giving!
    Melting our hearts into rivers of love;
Secret of life and the sweetness of living,
    Joy felt on earth that will fill us above.

Service of Jesus! Oh, service of praising!
    Such as redeemed ones, rejoicing, can sing,
Daily and hourly their voices upraising,
    Lauding their Saviour, extolling their King.
      – Eva Travers Poole

Chapter 5

Don't Be Found Wanting

Belshazzar the king held a great feast for a thousand of his nobles, and he was drinking wine in the presence of the thousand.
– Daniel 5:1

For twenty long years or more, we lose sight of Daniel. He may have been living in retirement for a portion of that time, but at the end of it he still appears to hold some appointment in the Babylonian court, although most likely a less prominent position than before. Nebuchadnezzar had died, and there was a young man whose name was Belshazzar ruling in Babylon or acting in some such position as regent.[5]

---

5   Reverting for a moment to Nebuchadnezzar, the fact that for a time, he shared in his father's kingly authority before becoming sole sovereign, explains some apparent difficulty as to dates. For example, Nebuchadnezzar is termed *king of Babylon* when he first laid siege to Jerusalem (Daniel 1:1; 2 Kings 24:1; 2 Chronicles 36:6). He carried Daniel and other captives away as hostages and returned to Babylon. He then commanded that the education and training of the four young Hebrews was to begin and allotted three years for

Some scholars believe that Belshazzar was admitted to a share of the sovereignty in conjunction with his father Nabonidus in much the same way as Nebuchadnezzar had reigned in association with his father. It is also believed that Nabonidus had recently fought a battle with Cyrus, but lost and took refuge in Borsippa. Consequently, Belshazzar was acting in his father's place, but what a time for revelry with a victorious enemy at the gates and his father shut up in a beleaguered fortress. This youthful ruler, however, *held a great feast for a thousand of his nobles, and he was drinking wine in the presence of the thousand.* We only get a single glimpse of this prince. This scene of the banquet is the first and last view we have of him, but it is enough.

How long that banqueting lasted we do not know, but in the East, feasts often extend over many days. Among the Jews, seven days was not an unusual time for the duration of a feast, and occasionally the time was extended to twice that, or fourteen days. It was a *great feast.* The king caroused with his governors and princes, his lords and the mighty men of Babylon, together with his wives and concubines, drinking and rioting and praising the *gods of gold and silver, of bronze, iron, wood and stone* (Daniel 5:4). That is more

---

that purpose. Three years are passed in their instruction, and they are then admitted into the order of the magi, or wise men (Daniel 1:5, 18; 2:2). And yet, although between three and four years have elapsed since the siege of Jerusalem, Nebuchadnezzar's dream is said to have occurred in the second year of his reign. There is a seeming discrepancy here. But let it be understood that the term *second year* in Daniel 2:1 refers to the time subsequent to his father's death, during which he had reigned alone, and the difficulty is removed.

or less what men are doing today, if they are bowing their knee to the god of this world.

Cyrus, the great Persian general, was outside the gates, besieging the city, just as Nebuchadnezzar had besieged Jerusalem. And this Belshazzar fancied himself secure behind the lofty and massive walls that encompassed Babylon.

The revelers become daring and reckless. They had forgotten the power of the God of the Hebrews, as shown in the days of Nebuchadnezzar. Heated with wine and lifted up with pride, they laid their sacrilegious hands on the golden vessels, which had been brought out of the temple of the house of God which was at Jerusalem, and they drank from those sacred cups. And as they drank to their idols, one can readily believe that they scoffed at the God of Israel. I could almost picture the scene before me and can imagine I hear them blaspheming His holy name. They made merry and were in the midst of their boisterous revelry.

But stop! What was the matter? The king was struck by something that he saw. His countenance changed, and he turned deathly pale. The wine cup fell from his grasp, and his knees shook. He trembled from head to foot. I wonder if maybe his lords and nobles secretly laughed at him, thinking he was drunk. But along the wall, standing out in living light, they saw letters of strange and unintelligible shape. *Suddenly the fingers of a man's hand emerged and began writing opposite the lampstand on the plaster of the wall of the king's palace, and the king saw the back of the hand that did the writing* (Daniel 5:5).

Above the golden candlestick,[6] on a bare space of the wall,[7] Belshazzar beheld that mysterious handwriting. He distinctly discerned the tracing of those terrible words. Was that writing on the palace wall the work of the same hand that had traced the tables of stone at Sinai? Or did some angelic messenger execute the divine commission? The words *fingers of a man's hand* seem to imply the latter.

The king cried aloud and commanded that the astrologers, the Chaldeans, and the soothsayers be brought forward. They came in and he said to them, *Any man who can read this inscription and explain its interpretation to me shall be clothed with purple and have a necklace of gold around his neck, and have authority as third ruler[8] in the kingdom* (Daniel 5:7).

One after another tried to spell out that writing, but they failed to understand it. They were skilled in Chaldean learning, but this inscription baffled them. They couldn't make out the meaning any more than an unrenewed man can make out the Bible. They did

---

6   Another writer said, "The fingers *wrote in front of the candlestick.* What candlestick? The candlestick of gold, with the lamps thereof, which Solomon had made was exhibited there in mockery and triumph, as its counterpart adorned the triumph of the Roman emperor ages later and was sculptured in bas-relief on ilie Arch of Titus, to be seen in Rome this very day." – *Daniel: Statesman and Prophet*, p. 160.

7   "The writing was traced on the plain plaster on the walls of the banquet room; as the prevailing taste for ornament, it is still found on the palaces of Nineveh. Those who have seen Mr. Layard's large and magnificent drawings of Assyrian antiquities will remember that elaborate decoration extends only to a certain height. Above that line the wall is quite plain and is, to this day, coated with lime." – *Daniel: Statesman and Prophet*, p. 160.

8   The *third ruler* – mark that! Belshazzar's father, Nabonidus, was probably the first; Belshazzar, the associate king, was the *second,* and the successful interpreter would be the *third.*

not understand God's writing; they could not comprehend it. A man must be born of the Spirit before he can understand God's Book or God's writing. No uncircumcised eyes could decipher those words of fire.

The queen[9] heard of the state of affairs and came to encourage and advise. She saluted the king with the words, *O king, live forever! Do not let your thoughts alarm you or your face be pale* (Daniel 5:10). Then she told him that there was one man in the kingdom who would be able to read the writing and tell its meaning. She proceeded to say that in the days of Nebuchadnezzar, *illumination, insight and wisdom like the wisdom of the gods were found in him* (Daniel 5:11). She advised him to summon Daniel.

> A man must be born of the Spirit before he can understand God's Book or God's writing.

For some years, Daniel may have been comparatively little known; he may have dropped out of sight. But now for the third time, he stood before a Babylonian ruler to interpret and to reveal, when the powers of the king's magicians and astrologers had utterly failed. Daniel came in, and his eyes lit up when he saw the letters upon the wall. He could read the meaning of the words. The king put forth his offer of rewards, but Daniel was not moved: *Keep your gifts for yourself or give your rewards to someone else; however, I will read the inscription to the king and make the interpretation known to him* (Daniel 5:17).

---

9   From the authority with which she speaks, it has been conjectured that this was the queen mother.

But before he read the words upon the wall, he gave the king a bit of his mind. Perhaps he had long been praying for an opportunity to warn him, and now he had it, and he wasn't going to let it slip away, even though all those mighty lords were there. So he reminded the king of the lessons he should have learned from the experience that fell upon the mighty Nebuchadnezzar – of how that monarch had been humbled, brought down, and deposed from his kingly throne, because *his heart was lifted up and his spirit became so proud that he behaved arrogantly,* until at length he came to repentance and *recognized that the Most High God is ruler over the realm of mankind* (Daniel 5:20-21). *Yet you, his son,*[10] *Belshazzar, have not humbled your heart, even though you knew all this, but you have exalted yourself against the Lord of heaven* (Daniel 5:22-23).

Then looking up at the mystic words standing forth in their brilliant light, he reads:

MENE, MENE, TEKEL, UPHARSIN

MENE; God has numbered your kingdom and put an end to it.

TEKEL; You have been weighed on the scales and found deficient.

PERES;[11] *Your kingdom has been divided and given over to the Medes and Persians* (Daniel 5:25-28).

---

10   Here, as in several other instances, *son* is used for *grandson,* and *father* is used for *grandfather.*

11   In interpreting, Daniel reads *PERES,* which is the singular form of the word of which *pharsin* is the plural. The *U* is the prefixed conjunction "and." – *Daniel: Statesman and Prophet,* pp. 171-172.

How the word of doom must have rung through the palace that night! That was an awful warning. Sinner, it is for you. What if God should put you in the balance, and you are without Christ? What would become of your soul? Take warning from Belshazzar's fate.

The destruction did not delay. The king thought he was perfectly secure; he thought the walls of Babylon were impregnable. But *that same night*, at the very hour when Daniel declared the doom of the king, Cyrus, the conquering Persian, turned the Euphrates from its regular course and channel and brought his army within those gigantic walls. The guard around the palace was beaten back, and the Persian soldiers forced their way to the banqueting hall. Belshazzar's blood flowed and mingled with the spilled wine upon the palace floor.

> O sinners, take the warning: Death and hell are near you.

It was Belshazzar's last night. One short chapter gives us all we know of that young monarch. His life was short. The wicked do not live out half their days. An impious young man, he had neglected or forgotten the holy Daniel; he had set aside his father's counselor and friend; he had turned away from the best adviser and most faithful servant that Nebuchadnezzar had ever had – the one who probably had done more than anyone else to build up and consolidate his kingdom. But this was his end.

O sinners, take the warning: Death and hell are near you – death and hell, I say. And it may be that they are just as close as was the sword of the slayer to those midnight revelers.

Chapter 6

Fearing God More than the Lions

All the commissioners of the kingdom, the prefects and the satraps, the high officials and the governors have consulted together that the king should establish a statute and enforce an injunction that anyone who makes a petition to any god or man besides you, O king, for thirty days, shall be cast into the lions' den.
– Daniel 6:7

In this chapter we find that Darius, who was probably one of the high military commanders engaged in the siege of Babylon, ruled the kingdom, while Cyrus was off conquering other parts of the world. As soon as Darius attained the throne, he made arrangements for governing the country. He divided the kingdom into 120 provinces, and he appointed a governor or ruler over each province, and over the governors he put three presidents to see that these rulers did not damage the king or swindle the government. And over these three presidents, he placed Daniel as president of the presidents.

Very possibly Darius knew of Daniel and considered him to be an able and conscientious statesman. Somehow the king either knew or was told enough about Daniel to justify his confidence in him. So Daniel was again in office. He held the highest position under the sovereign that anyone could hold in that day. He was next to the throne. If you will allow me the expression, he was the Bismarck or the Gladstone of the empire. He was prime minister; he was secretary of state, and all important matters had to pass through his hands.

We do not know how long he held that position, but sooner or later the other presidents and the governors grew jealous and wanted Daniel out of the way. It was as if they had said, "Let us see if we can't get this sanctimonious Hebrew removed; he has bossed us long enough." You see, he was so upright, they could do nothing with him. There were plenty of collectors and treasurers, but he kept such a close eye on them that they only made their salaries. There was no chance of plundering the government while he was at the head. He was president, and probably all the revenue accounts passed before him.

No doubt these enemies wanted to form an alliance, *For, behold, the wicked bend the bow, they make ready their arrow upon the string to shoot in darkness at the upright in heart* (Psalm 11:2). They may have talked somewhat like this: "If it were not for this man, we could form an alliance; then, in three or four years, we could make enough to enable us to retire from office and have a villa on the banks of the Euphrates, or we could go down to Egypt and see more of the world. We could have plenty of money – all we would ever want, or our children either – if we could just get control of the government and manage things as we like to. The way things are now, we only get our exact dues, and it will take years and years for them to amount to anything respectable. If we had matters in our own hands, it would be different, for King Darius does not know half as much about the affairs of this empire as does this old Hebrew. He watches our accounts so closely that we can't get any advantage over the government. Down with this pious Jew!"

Perhaps they worked matters to get an investigating committee, hoping to catch him in his accounts. But it was no use. If he had put any relatives in office unfairly, it would have been found out. And if he had been guilty of embezzlement or broken the unalterable laws of the kingdom, the matter would have come to light.

One of the highest eulogies ever paid to a man on earth was pronounced upon Daniel at this time by his enemies. These men were connected with the various parts of the kingdom, but when they put their heads together, they came to this conclusion: *they could find no ground of accusation or evidence of corruption, inasmuch as he was faithful, and no negligence or corruption was to be found in him. . . . We will not find any ground of accusation against this Daniel unless we find it against him with regard to the law of his God* (Daniel 6:4-5).

What a testimony from his bitterest enemies! If only that could be said of all of us. He had never taken a bribe; he had never been connected with an alliance; he had never put a friend into some lucrative office with the design of sharing the plunder and enriching himself. If he had been guilty in any of these things, these scrutineers would have found out. They had a keen scent for impropriety; they were sharp men; they knew all about his actions and his history. They would have been glad to have found something – anything – which would have led to his removal from his high position. But with much regret, they said, "We shall not find any occasion against him."

Ah, how his name shone. He had shone in his early manhood, and he had shone all along. He knew that *a good name is better than a good ointment* (Ecclesiastes 7:1). Now he was an old man, an old statesman, and yet this was their testimony. There had been no sacrifice of principle in order to gain votes, no buying up of men's votes or men's consciences, no "counting in" or "counting out." There had been none of that. He had walked straight from the beginning.

Character is worth more than money.

Young man, character is worth more than money. *He who walks in integrity walks securely, but he who perverts his ways will be found out* (Proverbs 10:9). Character is worth more than anything else in the whole wide world. I would rather have the character that Daniel's enemies attributed to him than have a monument of gold raised over my dead body that reached from earth to sky. I would rather have a testimony like that credited to Daniel than have all that this world can give.

The men said, "We will get him out of the way. We will get the king to sign a decree, and we will propose a penalty. It shall not be the fiery furnace this time. We will have a lions' den – a den of angry lions; they will soon do away with him." These plotters probably met at night, because most generally, if men want to do any downright-mean business, they meet at night; darkness suits them best. The chief president himself was not there, for he had not been invited to meet them. Very likely some lawyer, who understood the laws of the Medes and Persians, stood up and said something like this: "Gentlemen, I have a plan that will work well, so we may get rid of this old Hebrew. You know he will not serve any but the God of Abraham and of Isaac."

We know that very well, and if a man had gone to Babylon in those days, he would not have had to ask if Daniel loved the God of the Bible. I pity any man who lives so that people have to ask, "Is he a Christian?" Let us so live that no one need ask that question about us. These men knew very well that Daniel worshipped none other than the God of the Bible, the God of the Hebrews, the God of Abraham, the God of Moses – the God who had brought His people Israel out of Egypt, through the Red Sea, and into the promised land. They knew that very well.

And these plotters said to one another, "Now, let's get Darius to sign a decree that if any man *shall make a petition to any god or man for thirty days*, except of the king, *he shall be cast into the lions' den*. And let us all keep perfectly quiet about this matter, so that it won't be known. We must not tell our wives, or the news may spread through the city, and Daniel might hear about it. He has more influence with the king than all the rest of us put together. The king will never sign the decree if he finds out what the objective is."

Then they may have said, "We must draw it so tight that Darius will not be able to get out of it after he has once signed it. We must make it so binding that if the king signs it, we shall have that Daniel in the lions' den, and we will take good care that the lions shall be hungry."

When the trap was ready, the conspirators came to the king and began their business with flattering speech: *King Darius, live for ever.* When people approach me with smooth and oily words, I know they have something else in mind; I know they have some purpose behind telling me I am a good man. Perhaps these plotters went on to tell the king how prosperous the realm was and how much the people thought of him. Then, perhaps, in the most plausible way, they told him that if he signed this decree, he would be remembered by their children's children, and it would be a memorial forever of his greatness and goodness.

"What is this decree that you wish me to sign?" And running his eye over the document, he might have said, "I don't see any objection to that."

And one of the governors said, *Now, O king, establish the injunction and sign the document so that it may not be changed, according to the law of the Medes and Persians, which may not be revoked* (Daniel 6:8).

The king answered, "Oh yes, the law of the Medes and Persians; that is it." He put his signature to the decree and sealed it with his seal. In the pleasure of granting the request of these governors, he thought nothing about Daniel, and the presidents and governors carefully refrained from jogging his memory. They had told the king a lie too, for they said, *All the commissioners of the kingdom, the prefects and the satraps, the high officials and the governors have consulted together that the king should establish a statute*, although the chief president knew nothing at all about it (Daniel 6:7).

They probably gave a long preamble and told him how popular he was and that he was liked better than Nebuchadnezzar or Belshazzar. They most likely tickled his vanity and told him that he was the most popular man that had ever reigned in Babylon. Then they may have gone on to tell him how fond they were of him and his rule, and that they had been consulting together about how to increase his popularity to make him more beloved. Then they told him of a plan that was almost sure to do it. They would point out that if no one called upon any god except him for thirty days, it would make him a god and render him the most popular monarch that had ever reigned in Babylon, and his name would be handed down to posterity. If he could get men to call upon his name for thirty days, they would probably continue and therefore permanently reckon him among the gods.

If you touch a man's vanity, he will do almost anything, and Darius was like most of the human race. They touched his vanity by intimating that this would make him great. He thought it was a very wise suggestion and agreed with them.

It was not only Daniel they were thus going to get out of the way, but also every conscientious Jew. There was not a true Jew in the whole of that wide empire who would bow down and worship Darius, and these men knew that. So they were going to sweep away in one stroke all the Jews who were true to their faith. They hated them.

And I want to tell you that the world does not love Christians today. The world will persecute a man if he attempts to live the life of a true Christian. The world is no friend to true grace. A man may live for the world and like the world and escape persecution. But if the world has nothing to say against you, it is a pretty sure sign that God doesn't have much to say for you; if you seek to live for Christ Jesus, you must go against the current of the world.

> If the world has nothing to say against you, it is a pretty sure sign that God doesn't have much to say for you.

So the presidents and governors were ready to let the news of the decree go forth, and it would not be long before it spread through the highways of Babylon. The men of the city knew Daniel; they knew that he would not vacillate. They knew that the old man with the gray locks would not turn to the right hand or the left; they knew that if his enemies caught him in that way, he would not deny his God or turn away from Him. They knew that he was going to be true to his God.

Daniel was not a sickly Christian of the nineteenth

century; he was not one of your weak-backed, weak-kneed Christians; he had moral stamina and courage. I can imagine that aged, white-haired secretary of state sitting at his table going over the accounts of some of these rulers of provinces. Some of the timid, frightened Hebrews might have come to him and said, "Oh Daniel, have you heard the latest news?"

"No. What is it?"

"What? Haven't you been to the king's palace this morning?"

"No, I have not been to the palace today. What is the matter?"

"Well, there is a conspiracy against you. Many of those princes have induced King Darius to sign a decree that if any man shall call upon any other god in his kingdom for thirty days, he shall be thrown to the lions. Their objective is to cast you into the den. Now if you can only leave for a little time, if you will just flee Babylon for thirty days, it will be better for you and the public. You are the chief secretary and treasurer; in fact, you are the principal member of the government. You are an important man and can do as you please. You should get out of Babylon now. Or, if you decide to stay in Babylon, do not let anyone catch you on your knees. In any case, do not pray at the window that faces Jerusalem, as you have been doing for the last fifty years. If you pray, close that window, draw a curtain over it, shut the door, and stop up every crevice. People are sure to be listening around your house."

Some of our nineteenth-century Christians would have advised Daniel in the same fashion: "Can't you find some important business to do in Egypt and take a journey to Memphis? Can't you think of something that needs to be looked after in Syria, so you can hurry off to Damascus? Or, surely you can say there is a need for you to go to Assyria, and you can visit Nineveh. Or why not go as far as Jerusalem to see what changes fifty or sixty years have made? Anyway, just leave Babylon for the next thirty days, so that your enemies cannot catch you. For, depend upon it, they will all be on the watch, and whatever you do, be sure they do not catch you on your knees."

Many men are ashamed to be caught upon their knees. Many a man, if found upon his knees by his devoted wife, will jump up and walk around the room as if he had no particular objective in mind. How many young men there are who come from the country and enter city life but do not have the moral courage to go down on their knees before their roommates.

How many young men say, "Don't ask me to get down on my knees at this prayer meeting." Men don't have the moral courage to be seen praying. They lack moral courage. Ah, thousands of men have been lost because of a lack of moral courage; they have been lost because at some critical moment they shrank from going to their knees and being seen and known as worshippers of God – as being on the Lord's side. The fact is that we are a pack of cowards; that is what we are. Shame on the Christianity of the nineteenth century! It is a weak and sickly thing. If only we had a host of men like Daniel living today.

I can picture that aged man Daniel with his gray

hair as he listened to the words of these miserable counselors, who would tempt him to condense, reduce, and change to save his skin at the cost of his conscience. But their counsel fell flat and dead. Imagine how Daniel would receive a suggestion that he should appear to be ashamed of the God of his fathers. Would he have been ashamed or afraid? Not likely! You know he would not, and I know he would not.

"They will be watching you; they will have their spies all around. But if you are determined to go on praying, shut your window, close your curtains, and stop up the keyhole, so that no one can look through and see you on your knees or overhear a single word. Accommodate yourself just a little. Compromise just a little."

That is the cry of the world today. It is, "Accommodate yourself to the times. Compromise just a little here, and deviate just a little there, to suit the opinions and views of a mocking world." Do you think that Daniel, after walking with God for half a century or more, would turn around like that? Ten thousand times, No!

True as steel, that old man went to his room three times a day. Take note, he had time to pray. Many a businessman today will tell you he has no time to pray; his business is so pressing that he cannot call his family around him and ask God to bless them. He is so busy that he cannot ask God to keep him and them from the temptations of the present life – the everyday temptations. "Business is so pressing."

I am reminded of the words of an old Methodist minister: "If you have so much business to attend to that you have no time to pray, you have more business than God ever intended you to have."

But look at this man. He had all, or nearly all, of the king's business to attend to. He was prime minister, secretary of state, and secretary of the treasury, all in one. He had to attend to all his own work and oversee the work of many other men. Yet he found time to pray – not just now and then, nor once in a while, or just when he happened to have a few moments to spare. Daniel *knelt on his knees three times a day, praying and giving thanks before his God, as he had been doing previously* (Daniel 6:10). Yes, he could take up the words of the fifty-fifth psalm, and say:

> *As for me, I shall call upon God, And the LORD will save me.*
>
> *Evening and morning and at noon, I will complain and murmur, and He will hear my voice.* (Psalm 55:16-17)

Busy as he was, he found time to pray. A man whose habit is to call upon God saves time instead of losing it. He has a clearer head and a more collected mind; he is able to act with more decision when circumstances require it. What men can't achieve on their own, God can cause to fall into place without hardly any effort on the man's part. God blesses those who love Him.

So Daniel went to his room three times a day; he trod that path so often that the grass could not grow on it. I am inclined to say those plotters knew where he would go to pray; they knew the place where Daniel's prayer would be made, and they were sure they could find him there at his usual hours. Once again he had a purpose firm and dared to make it known.

He went to pray as before *in his roof chamber he had windows open toward Jerusalem* (Daniel 6:10). Like Paul in later days, he knew whom he had believed; like Moses, he saw Him who is invisible (2 Timothy 1:12; Hebrews 11:27). He knew whom he worshipped. There was no need to trace back the church records for years to find out whether this man had ever made a profession of faith.

> It is right to pray for our rulers.

He was not careful to inquire whether there were any outsiders or whether they could hear. In tones not one atom softer or quieter than was his custom, he poured out his prayer to the God of his life – to the God of his people, the God of Abraham, Isaac, and Jacob. He even prayed for the king. It is right to pray for our rulers.

Paul wrote to Timothy, *First of all, then, I urge that entreaties and prayers, petitions and thanksgivings, be made on behalf of all men, for kings and all who are in authority, so that we may lead a tranquil and quiet life in all godliness and dignity* (1 Timothy 2:1-2). If we cease praying for our rulers, our country will go to pieces. The reason they are often not better is that we do not pray for them. Does Daniel pray to Darius? No, he prayed *for* Darius but not *to* him.

Men listened near Daniel's open window; the 120 princes took care of that. They themselves were their own witnesses, and some of them gathered together as listeners to do their own vile work. If there had been any newspaper reporters in that day, they would have been anxious to get every word of that prayer. If they had the smallest chance, they would have written it down and telegraphed it all over the world within twenty-four hours.

After Daniel had prayed and given thanks, he was undaunted. If it was the will of God that he pass from earth to heaven by way of the lions' den, he was prepared. God's presence was with him. Like Enoch, he bore within himself this testimony – *that he was pleasing to God* (Hebrews 11:5).

Do You See the Hebrew Captive Kneeling

Do you see the Hebrew captive kneeling,
    At morning, noon, and night, to pray?
In his chamber he remembers Zion,
    Though in exile far away.

Do not fear to tread the fiery furnace,
    Nor shrink the lions' den to share;
For the God of Daniel will deliver,
    He will send His angel there.

Children of the living God, take courage,
    Your great deliverance sweetly sing.
Set your faces toward the hill of Zion,
    Thence to hail your coming King.

Are your windows open toward Jerusalem,
    Though as captives here, a "little while" we stay?
For the coming of the King in His glory
    Are you watching day by day?
        – Philip P. Bliss

Chapter 7

Godliness Wins in the End

Then the king gave orders, and Daniel was brought in and cast into the lions' den. – Daniel 6:16

There must have been great excitement in the city at that time, for all Babylon knew that this man would not falter. They knew this old statesman was a man with an iron will, and it was not likely he would yield. The lions' den had few terrors to him. He would rather be in the lions' den with God than out of it without Him.

And it is a thousand times better, friends, to be in the lions' den with God and hold to our principles than to be out of it and have money but no principles. I pity those men who have gained their money dishonestly; I pity those men who have obtained their positions in life dishonestly; I pity any politician who has acquired his office dishonestly. How their consciences lash them!

And how the Word of God lashes such men. *Your gold and your silver have rusted; and their rust will be a witness against you and will consume your flesh like fire* (James 5:3). It does not pay to be false; it pays to be true. It is best to be honest, even if it means having little money in our pocket and little position in the world. It is best to have God with us and to know that we are on the right side.

I venture to say that Daniel was worth more than any other man Darius had in his empire – yes, worth more than forty thousand men who wanted to get him out of the way. He was true to the king. He prayed for him; he loved him, and he did for that king everything he could that did not conflict with the law of his God.

It does not pay to be false; it pays to be true.

And now the spies rushed to the king and cried, "O *King Darius, live for ever.* Do you know there is a man in your kingdom who will not obey you?"

"A man who won't obey me! Who is he?"

"Why, that man Daniel. That Hebrew whom you set over us. He persists in calling upon his God."

And the moment they mentioned the name of Daniel, a frown arose upon the king's brow, and the thought flashed into his mind, "Ah, I have made a mistake; I should never have signed that decree. I should have known that Daniel would never call upon me. I know whom he serves; he serves the God of his fathers." So, instead of blaming Daniel, he blamed himself; instead of condemning Daniel, he condemned himself. Then he labored to determine how he could manage to preserve Daniel unharmed.

All that day, if you could have looked into the palace, you would have seen the king walking up and down the halls and corridors, greatly troubled with the thought that this man must lose his life before the sun set on that Chaldean plain, for if Daniel were not in the lions' den by sundown, the law of the Medes and Persians would be broken, and come what may, that law had to be observed and kept.

Darius loved Daniel, and in his heart he sought to deliver him. All day he pursued a plan by which he might save Daniel but still preserve the Median law unbroken. But he did not love Daniel as much as your King loves you; he did not love him as much as Christ loves us, for if he had, he would have proposed to go into the lions' den in Daniel's place. Let us remember that Christ tasted death for us. *But we do see Him who was made for a little while lower than the angels, namely, Jesus, because of the suffering of death crowned with glory and honor, so that by the grace of God He might taste death for everyone* (Hebrews 2:9).

Those plotters must have had a suspicion about the king's feelings, so they said, "If you break the law which you yourself have made, respect for the laws of the Medes and Persians will be gone. Your subjects will no longer obey you, and your kingdom will depart from you." So Darius was compelled to forsake Daniel; he spoke the word for the officers to seize him and take him to the den. Daniel's enemies took care that the den was filled with the hungriest beasts in Babylon.

You might have seen those officers going out to bind that old man with the white, flowing hair; they might have marched to his dwelling and bound his hands together. Those Chaldean soldiers led captive the man who ranked next to the king a few hours earlier – the noblest statesman Babylon had ever possessed. They guarded him along the way that led to the lions' den. As he was led along the streets, he walked with a firm and steady step, bearing himself like a conqueror. He didn't tremble. His knees were firm and didn't knock together.

The light of heaven shone in his calm face, and all heaven was interested in that aged man. Disgraced on earth, he was probably the most popular man in heaven. Angels delighted in him; how they loved him up there! He had stood firm; he had not deviated; he had not turned away from the God of the Bible. And he walked with a giant's stride to the entrance of the lions' den, where they cast him in. They rolled a great stone to the mouth of the den, and the king put his seal upon it. And so, the law was kept.

Daniel was cast into the den, but the angel of God came down, and God's servant remained unharmed. The lions' mouths were stopped, and they were as harmless as lambs. If you had looked into that den, you would have seen a man as calm as a summer evening. I do not doubt that at his usual hour of prayer, he knelt down as if he had been in his own chamber, and if he could have had the points of the compass in that den, he would have prayed with his face toward Jerusalem. He loved that city; he loved the temple. He probably prayed and gave thanks with his face toward the city of Jerusalem. I can imagine him laying his head on one of the lions and going to sleep. If that were so, no one in Babylon slept more sweetly than Daniel in the den of lions.

But there was one man in Babylon who had no rest that night. If you could have looked into the king's palace, you would have seen one man in great trouble. *Then the king went off to his palace and spent the night fasting, and no entertainment was brought before him; and his sleep fled from him* (Daniel 6:18). Darius did not have his musicians play for him that night. Away with music and singing! There was no feast that night; he could eat nothing. The servants brought him dainty food, but he had no appetite for it. He felt troubled; he could not sleep. He had put the best man in his kingdom in that den of lions, and he faulted himself for it. He might have said to himself, "How could I have been a party to such an act as that?"

And early in the morning, probably in the grey dawn before the sun had risen, the men of Babylon could have heard the wheels of the king's chariot rolling over the pavement. King Darius drove in haste to the lions' den. He would have dismounted from his chariot in eager haste and cried into the mouth of the den, *Daniel, servant of the living God, has your God, whom you constantly serve, been able to deliver you from the lions?* (Daniel 6:20).

Hark! A voice answered, and it was like a resurrection voice; from the depths it came up to the king's ear, and he heard the words of Daniel: *O king, live for ever! My God sent His angel and shut the lions' mouths and they have not harmed me, inasmuch as I was found innocent before Him; and also toward you, O king, I have committed no crime* (Daniel 6:21-22).

The lions could not harm him. The very hairs of his head were numbered. Whenever a man stands by God, God will stand by him. It was well for Daniel that he did not falter. Oh, how his name shines. What a blessed character he was.

The king gave the command that Daniel should be taken up out of the den. *So Daniel was taken up out of the den and no injury whatever was found on him, because he had trusted in his God* (Daniel 6:23). As he reached the top, I think they must have embraced one another, and then maybe Daniel mounted the king's chariot and was driven back to the royal palace. There were two happy men in Babylon that morning. Maybe they sat down for a meal together, thankful and rejoicing.

Whenever a man stands by God, God will stand by him.

No injury whatever was found on him. The God who had preserved Shadrach, Meshach, and Abednego in the fiery furnace, so that no *smell of fire had passed on them*, had preserved Daniel from the jaws of the lions.

But Daniel's accusers fared very differently. As the proverb says, *He who digs a pit will fall into it* (Proverbs 26:27). The king ordered Daniel's accusers to be delivered to the same situation, so they were cast into the den, and *the lions overpowered them and crushed all their bones* (Daniel 6:24). *For the LORD loves justice and does not forsake His godly ones; They are preserved*

forever, but the descendants of the wicked will be cut off
(Psalm 37:28).

Young men, let us come out from the world; let us
trample it under our feet; let us be true to God; let us
stand in rank, and keep step, and fight boldly for our
King. Then our "crowning time" shall come by and
by. Yes, the reward will come, and then it may be said
of one or another of us: *O man of high esteem* (Daniel
10:19). Young men, your moral character is more than
money. It is worth more than the honor of the world,
which is fleeting and will soon be gone. It is worth more
than earthly position, which is transient and will soon
be gone. But to have God with you and to be with God
– what a grand position! It is an eternal inheritance.

A few more words about Daniel: If you look at the
tenth chapter, you will read that an angel came to him
and told him he was a *man of high esteem*. Another
angel had brought him a similar message on a previ-
ous occasion. Many are of the opinion that the one
described in the tenth chapter as appearing to Daniel
is none other than the one *like a Son of man*, who vis-
ited John when he was banished to the Isle of Patmos
(Revelation 1:13). People thought that John was sent
to that island by himself, but no, the angel of God was
with him. And so it was with Daniel – taken from his
own country and his own people. In this chapter we
read, *I lifted my eyes and looked, and behold, there was
a certain man dressed in linen, whose waist was girded
with a belt of pure gold: . . . He said to me, "O Daniel,
man of high esteem, understand the words that I am*

about to tell you and stand upright , for I have now been sent to you" (Daniel 10:5, 11).

It was Daniel's need that brought this angel from the glory land. And it was the Son of God by his side in that city of Babylon. As I said before, that was the second time word had come to him that he was *of high esteem.* Yes, a messenger came from the throne of God to tell him this three separate times.

Note the precious verse in the eleventh chapter: *the people who know their God will display strength and take action* (Daniel 11:32). Two verses of the twelfth chapter also speak blessings for the righteous: *Many of those who sleep in the dust of the ground will awake, these to everlasting life, but the others to disgrace and everlasting contempt. Those who have insight will shine brightly like the brightness of the expanse of heaven, and those who lead the many to righteousness, like the stars forever and ever* (Daniel 12:2-3).

This was the consolation the angel gave Daniel, and what a great consolation it was. The fact concerning all of us is that we like to shine. There is no doubt about that. Every mother likes her child to shine. If her son shines at school by getting to the head of his class, the proud mother tells all the neighbors, and I suppose she has a right to do so. But the great ones of this world will not be the ones to shine the brightest. For a few years they may shed bright light, but they go out in darkness; they have no inner light. Shining for a time, they go out in the blackness of darkness. Where are the great men who did not know Daniel's God? How long did they shine? We know little of Nebuchadnezzar and the rest, except as they fill in the story about these humble men of God. We are not told that statesmen will shine; they may for a few days or years, but they are soon forgotten.

Look at those great ones who passed away in the days of Daniel. How wise in council they were! How mighty and victorious over many nations! What gods upon earth they were! Yet their names are forgotten and written in the sand. What about the so-called philosophers? Do they live? Behold men of science, archaeologists, and scientific men, who go down into the bowels of the earth and hammer away at some rock, trying to make it talk against the voice of God. They shall die by and by, and their names shall rot.

But the man of God shines. Yes, he is the one who shall shine as the stars forever and ever. This Daniel has been gone for twenty-five hundred years, but increasing millions read of his life and actions. And so it shall be to the end of time. He will only become better known and better loved; he will only shine brighter as the world grows older. Of a truth, *those that understand shall shine . . . and . . . teach righteousness to the multitude as the stars in perpetual eternity.*

And this blessed happiness of shining in the glory is like all the blessings of God's kingdom for everyone, as He *has blessed us with every spiritual blessing in the heavenly places in Christ* (Ephesians 1:3). Even without the least claim to education or refinement, you can shine. A poor working man or a poor sailor can shine forever, if he works for the kingdom of God. The Bible does not say the great shall shine, but *those that teach righteousness.*

Many of God's people have a false impression that only a few can speak for God. If anything is to be done for the souls of men, nine-tenths of the people say, "Oh, the ministers must do it." It does not enter into the minds of many people that they have a part in the matter. The devil works to keep Christians from the blessed privilege of winning souls to God. Anyone can do this work.

Don't you see how that little mountain brook keeps swelling until it carries everything downstream? Little trickling streams run into it until it becomes a mighty river; it has great cities on its banks, and the commerce of all nations floating on its waters. So when a single soul is won to Christ, you cannot see the result, but a single soul multiplies to a thousand and the thousand into ten thousand. Perhaps a million will be the fruit. We don't know. We only know that the Christian who has turned many to righteousness shall indeed shine forever and ever. Look at those poor, unlettered fishermen, the disciples of Jesus. They were not learned men, but they were great in winning souls. There is not a child who cannot work for God. *For we are His workmanship, created in Christ Jesus for good works, which God prepared beforehand so that we would walk in them* (Ephesians 2:10).

The one thing that keeps people from working for God is that they don't have the desire to do it. If a man has this desire, God soon qualifies him. And what we want is God's qualification; it must come from Him.

In our large meetings, there are frequently three thousand Christians present. If these were living in communion with Christ, is it too much to expect that they should each lead one soul to the Lord within a month? The Son of God gave His life for them. Should they refuse to work for Him when He supplies the needed power? What results should we see in souls saved if everyone did his or her work?

How many times have I watched at the close of a meeting to see if Christians would speak to the sorrowing ones. If we only had open-eyed watchers for souls, there would be multitudes of inquirers where now there are only individual cases. Every church would need an inquiry meeting after every gospel service, and these rooms would be crowded.

> Let the prayer of every Christian be, "Oh God, give me souls for my hire."

These searchers are at every meeting, anxious to have warm-hearted Christians lead them to Christ. They are timid but will always listen to someone speaking to them about Christ. Let the prayer of every Christian be, "Oh God, give me souls for my hire." What would be the result if this were the case with us? Multitudes would send up shouts of praise to God and make heaven glad. *There is joy in the presence of the angels of God over one sinner who repents* (Luke 15:10). Where there is an anxious sinner, there is a place for the Christian.

What Art Thou Doing?

What art *thou* doing, Christian?
    Is it work for Christ thy Lord?
Art thou winning many sinners
    By thy life, thy pen, thy word?
When the solemn question cometh,
    What will thine answer be?
Canst thou point to something finished,
    Saying, "Lord, my work for Thee?"

What doest thou in service –
    Art thou taking active part?
Are life and tongue in earnest
    Outflow of loving heart?
Or art thou idly gazing
    While others toil and sow,
Content with simply praising
    The earnestness they show?

What doest thou, redeemed one,
    Child of a mighty King?
What glory to thy Father
    Doth thy princely bearing bring?
If no one brought Him honour,
    And no one gave Him praise,
To thee it appertaineth
    The paean-note to raise.

What doest thou here? Wherever
    Thine earthly lot be cast,
Oh, let each hour and moment
    In gladsome work be past.
Here! thou may'st do a life-work,
    Here! thou may'st win a crown,
Starlit and gem-surrounded,
    To cast before the throne.
        – Eva Travers Poole

Dwight L. Moody – A Brief Biography

Dwight Lyman Moody was born on February 5, 1837, in Northfield, Massachusetts. His father died when Dwight was only four years old, leaving his mother with nine children to care for. When Dwight was seventeen years old, he left for Boston to work as a salesman. A year later, he was led to Jesus Christ by Edward Kimball, Moody's Sunday school teacher. Moody soon left for Chicago and began teaching a Sunday school class of his own. By the time he was twenty-three, he had become a successful shoe salesman, earning $5,000 in only eight months, which was a lot of money for the middle of the nineteenth century. Having decided to follow Jesus, though, he left his career to engage in Christian work for only $300 a year.

D. L. Moody was not an ordained minister, but was an effective evangelist. He was once told by Henry Varley, a British evangelist, "Moody, the world has yet to see what God will do with a man fully consecrated to Him."

Moody later said, "By God's help, I aim to be that man."

It is estimated that during his lifetime, without the help of television or radio, Moody traveled more than one million miles, preached to more than one million people, and personally dealt with over seven hundred and fifty thousand individuals.

D. L. Moody died on December 22, 1899.

Moody once said, "Some day you will read in the papers that D. L. Moody, of East Northfield, is dead. Don't you believe a word of it! At that moment I shall be more alive than I am now. I shall have gone up higher, that is all – out of this old clay tenement into a house that is immortal; a body that death cannot touch, that sin cannot taint, a body fashioned like unto His glorious body. I was born of the flesh in 1837. I was born of the Spirit in 1856. That which is born of the flesh may die. That which is born of the Spirit will live forever."

Similar Updated Classics

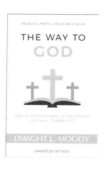

The Way to God, by Dwight L. Moody

There is life in Christ. Rich, joyous, wonderful life. It is true that the Lord disciplines those whom He loves and that we are often tempted by the world and our enemy, the devil. But if we know how to go beyond that temptation to cling to the cross of Jesus Christ and keep our eyes on our Lord, our reward both here on earth and in heaven will be 100 times better than what this world has to offer.

This book is thorough. It brings to life the love of God, examines the state of the unsaved individual's soul, and analyzes what took place on the cross for our sins. *The Way to God* takes an honest look at our need to repent and follow Jesus, and gives hope for unending, joyous eternity in heaven.

Available where books are sold.

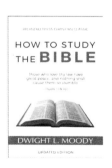

How to Study the Bible,
by Dwight L. Moody

There is no situation in life for which you cannot find some word of consolation in Scripture. If you are in affliction, if you are in adversity and trial, there is a promise for you. In joy and sorrow, in health and in sickness, in poverty and in riches, in every condition of life, God has a promise stored up in His Word for you.

This classic book by Dwight L. Moody brings to light the necessity of studying the Scriptures, presents methods which help stimulate excitement for the Scriptures, and offers tools to help you comprehend the difficult passages in the Scriptures. To live a victorious Christian life, you must read and understand what God is saying to you. Moody is a master of using stories to illustrate what he is saying, and you will be both inspired and convicted to pursue truth from the pages of God's Word.

Available where books are sold.

The Overcoming Life, by Dwight L. Moody

Are you an overcomer? Or, are you plagued by little sins that easily beset you? Even worse, are you failing in your Christian walk, but refuse to admit and address it? No Christian can afford to dismiss the call to be an overcomer. The earthly cost is minor; the eternal reward is beyond measure.

Dwight L. Moody is a master at unearthing what ails us. He uses stories and humor to bring to light the essential principles of successful Christian living. Each aspect of overcoming is looked at from a practical and understandable angle. The solution Moody presents for our problems is not religion, rules, or other outward corrections. Instead, he takes us to the heart of the matter and prescribes biblical, God-given remedies for every Christian's life. Get ready to embrace genuine victory for today, and joy for eternity.

Available where books are sold.

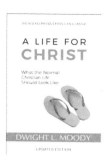

A Life for Christ, by Dwight L. Moody

In the church today, we have everything buttoned up perfectly. The music is flawless, the sermon well-prepared and smoothly delivered, and the grounds meticulously kept. People come on time and go home on time. But a fundamental element is missing. The business of church has undermined the individual's need to truly live for Christ, so much so, that only a limited few are seeing their life impact the world.

Dwight L. Moody takes us deep into Scripture and paints a clear picture of what ought to be an individual's life for Christ. The call for each Christian is to become an active member in the body of Christ. The motive is love for the Lord and our neighbor. The result will be the salvation of men, women, and children everywhere.

Available where books are sold.

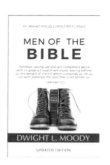

Men of the Bible, by Dwight L. Moody

When you wish to know something about godly living, where do you look? Is there a better place to look than to the men of the Bible? The Lord, in all His wisdom, left us with a wonderful textbook – the Holy Scriptures.

Some make the mistake of worshiping these heroes of the faith. Others make the mistake of only highlighting these men's weaknesses. Somewhere in the middle, though, is what God intended, and if our heart is right, we can learn all we need to know about healthy, rewarding Christian living from these incredible men of the Lord.

Available where books are sold.